GOLFERS ON GOLF

GOLFERS ON GOLF

Witty, Colorful and Profound Quotations on the Game of Golf

Selected & Edited by
Downs MacRury

Foreword by
Peter Jacobsen

Signature Press Editions™
Published by World Publications Group, Inc.
140 Laurel Street
East Bridgewater, MA 02333
www.wrldpub.net

ISBN 978-1-57215-007-2
ISBN 1-57215-007-6

Printed and bound in China by SNP Leefung Printers Limited.

1 2 3 4 5   06 05 03 02

TABLE OF CONTENTS

Foreword

Golf is like life—we can't control it, but if we apply our will, our commitment and whatever talent we have, we can get better at it. But, *best of all*, golf is supposed to be fun. Intelligent, challenging, frustrating fun. I think people are attracted to the game because it's one of the few things that can reward a person for the time spent with it. And nowhere else in life can someone accurately track their improvement so satisfyingly.

Along our various golfing journeys, we get the opportunity to meet a fascinating cross-section of humanity: the joyful and the talented, the hopeful and the pessimistic, the patient and the "golf-club-shattering." Golf can teach us about ourselves if we listen, and about others if we watch.

In my book, *Buried Lies*, I attempted to cover some of the emotional, even spiritual, aspects of golf. *Golfers on Golf* touches on these topics too, but it's really a cornucopia of observations, insightful and philosophical, practical and silly, unexpected and timeless, written and spoken by those with a lifetime invested in golf. You'll find all this, and more, in *Golfers on Golf*. Congratulations to the author, Downs MacRury, for capturing golf's myriad, magnificent and amusing possibilities.

Peter Jacobsen

Introduction

George Plimpton once posited an interesting theory: that there exists an inverse correlation between the size of the ball and the quality of writing about the sport in which the ball is used. Thus golf and baseball are the two sports where we find the best writing and, not inconsequentially, the largest number of readers. Given golf's demographics and diminutive ball circumference, is it really a surprise that the late Harvey Penick's little red tome is the largest selling book in sports publishing history?

Probably not, much to the envy of eye-strained wretches (aka writers) around the globe. Doubtless, pro athlete manque Plimpton would find pleasure in the Penick family's semi-annual royalty statements. But *Golfers on Golf* is less a covetous attempt to revisit publishing lightning-in-a-bottle (though, yes, I'll admit to some of that) than an effort to address a perceived need in the literature of golf. For, surprisingly, there are few sophisticated books of quotes on golf. And none, that I can find, exclusively devoted to the golfers themselves. (Golfers are herein defined as anyone who loves and plays the game. Though the great majority of quotes will be from professional golfers, passionate amateurs of all stripes and handicaps are included.)

Golfers on Golf wants to be something different and special; witty is fine but there's also the concise and poignant, the idiosyncratic and the substantive, the wry and the profound, the delightful and surprising and occasionally the heart-warming.

In selecting the quotations for *Golfers on Golf*, I've attempted to keep in mind what I believe golfers and readers want most in a collection of quotations: they want to be surprised, entertained and, I believe, inspired. Why the latter? Because inspiration reminds us why we love something or someone in the first place. Inspiration refreshes our memory.

Golfers on Golf is a celebration of a shared passion for the game of golf, a passion that, in its intensity, is unique, enduring and addictive.

Downs MacRury
Marina del Rey, CA

Dedication

For Alexandra May and Sean Edward, my niece and nephew ... may they tear up the golf course with as much relish as they tear up the living room.

Acknowledgments

I'd like to thank Carl Waldman, captain of the 1965 Friends School (NY) Golf Team, and Peter Rosenblatt, a recent golfing convert (and zealot-in-the-making), for their dedicated, all-consuming passion in researching the sport's vast literature. I couldn't have completed this book without them, nor would I have wanted to.

Thanks as well to Tim Snow, my pal and television producer extraordinaire, for showing me what true courage looks like.

And to my partner in golf and life, Maggie Begley, my heartfelt gratitude for allowing me the occasional mulligan. My goal is to reduce same to two a round ... or week.

It is almost impossible to remember how tragic a place the world is when one is playing golf.

Robert Lynd

Bon Mots

Worst swing I ever heard.

Charlie Boswell—a blind golfer after a player's mis-hit

If a lot of people gripped a knife and fork like they do a golf club, they'd starve to death.

Sam Snead

He's the only golfer in history who has become a living legend in his spare time.

Chi Chi Rodriguez—on Jack Nicklaus's infrequent tournament appearances

I have a tip that can take five strokes off anyone's golf game. It's called an eraser.

Arnold Palmer

If you are going to throw a club, it is important to throw it ahead of you, down the fairway, so you don't waste energy going back to pick it up.

Tommy Bolt

I'm hitting the woods just great, but I'm having a terrible time getting out of them.

Harry Toscano

I can airmail the golf ball, but sometimes I don't put the right address on it.

Jim Dent

I don't like number 4 balls. And I don't like fives, sixes or sevens on my cards.

George Archer

Nothing goes down slower than a golf handicap.

Bobby Nichols

The next one.

Ben Hogan—on being asked by Bob Toski what
he thought was the most important shot

Still your shot.

Dave Marr—golf's three ugliest words

The worst club in my bag is my brain.

Chris Perry

Slow is long, fast is short.

Don January

My old name was fine for a violin player but lousy for a golfer.
Gene Sarazen—on being asked why he changed
his name from Eugene Saraceni

Golf swings are like snowflakes: there are no two exactly alike.
Peter Jacobsen

Under an assumed name.
Dutch Harrison—to an annoying duffer who asked
Harrison's advice on how to play a shot

I've been squeezing the club so hard the cow is screaming.
J.C. Snead

I can't understand why people say Ben is so untalkative. He speaks to me on every green. He says, "You're away."
Jimmy Demaret—on taciturn Ben Hogan

A golf ball is like a clock. Always hit it at 6 o'clock and make it go toward 12 o'clock. Just be sure you're in the same time zone.
Chi Chi Rodriguez

It just happened that the hole got in the way. I was trying to make a 4 and made a 3.

Fuzzy Zoeller

You don't have to talk, just listen.

Lee Trevino—to Tony Jacklin, after Jacklin told him he didn't want to talk during a round

My swing is so bad I look like a caveman killing his lunch.

Lee Trevino

My career started slowly, then tapered off.

Gary McCord

Golf is the most fun you can have without taking your clothes off.

Chi Chi Rodriguez

It hit a spectator, but the ball's okay.

Jerry Pate—on a gallery shot

Man, I can't even point that far.

Gay Brewer—on a drive by John Daly

The rest of the field.

Roger Maltbie—on being asked what he would have to shoot to win

Ben, we're all proud of you. You've started a trend. We're all going to go out tonight and see if we can get hit by a bus.

Tommy Bolt—after Ben Hogan's win in the 1950 U.S. Open (the previous year he was nearly killed in a collision with a bus)

Ninety percent of this game is half mental.

Jim Wohlford

He's like a young Toots Shor—a victim of circumference.

Jimmy Demaret—on young Jack Nicklaus

It's not whether you win or lose, but whether I win or lose.

Sandy Lyle

Golf is an awkward set of bodily contortions designed to produce a graceful result.

Tommy Armour

The pivot is the utilization of multiple centers to produce a circular motion for generating centrifugal force on an adjusted plane, plus the maintenance of balance necessary to promote the two-line delivery path.

J.C. Andersen—delivered with a straight face

I wish I had kept my damned mouth shut.

Jack Nicklaus—on losing the 1971 U.S. Open to Lee Trevino during which he had given him words of encouragement

Two balls in the water! By God, I've got a good mind to jump in and make it four!

Simon Hobday

Madam, I believe that moderation is essential in all things, but never in my life have I been beaten by a teetotaler.

Harry Vardon—on being asked by a leader of the Women's Christian Temperance Union to sign a pledge to give up drinking

I'm not saying God himself couldn't have gotten my first shot out, but He would have had to throw it out.

Arnold Palmer—after needing five strokes to get out of a hole at Muirfield in the 1987 British Open

There's just no way to make the hole look bigger.

Tommy Armour

Take off two weeks, then quit the game.

Jimmy Demaret—to a struggling golfer

You know, if this wasn't my living, I wouldn't do this if you paid me.

> *Christy O'Connor Jr.—after getting rained*
> *out on a round*

Like watching paint dry.

> *Curtis Strange—describing his own game*

One bad shot does not make a losing score.

> *Gay Brewer*

I'd like to be known as a gentleman first, and then as a golfer. That's all.

> *Ben Hogan—on being asked how he'd like to be remembered*

I thought it was a new golf course.

> *Sandy Lyle—on being asked what he thought of an*
> *up-and-coming amateur named Tiger Woods*

Colleagues

When I joined the tour, I studied the best players to see what they didn't do. I came to the conclusion that the successful players had the Three Cs: Confidence. Composure. Concentration.

Bob Toski

Unlike some people, I try not to criticize a golfer who has attention-getting mannerisms. I think golf needs colorful players.

Gary Player

I've just watched a kid who doesn't know anything about playing golf, and I don't want to be around when he learns how.

Gene Sarazen—after seeing Sam Snead play for the first time

He has milked more success out of his natural ability than any other athlete I know.

Sam Snead—on Gary Player

Tommy [Bolt] may lose his temper a bit, but it doesn't bother me because he never interferes with my play. The only person he hurts is himself.

Gary Player

The best sand player I have ever seen is, without doubt, Gary Player ... Playing against him, you begin hoping he'll be on grass rather than in sand anytime he misses a green.

Jack Nicklaus

He combined grace, force, and brute strength in an unnatural motion that seemed perfectly suited to his personality.

Peter Jacobsen—on Arnold Palmer

To go against Jack Nicklaus, to go against the greatest player who ever played in my opinion, and to win, that has to be the greatest thrill for any golfer. It is my greatest thrill in golf.

Tom Watson—after beating Nicklaus in the '77 British Open

One of the best I've seen at keeping his routine constant in the most critical situations is Lee Trevino. He takes the same amount of time and makes the same moves for a shot that will win him a major championship as he does in a practice round.

Al Geiberger

If we could have screwed another head on his shoulders, he would have been the greatest golfer that ever lived.

Ben Hogan—on Tommy Bolt

If Jimmy [Demaret] had concentrated on golf as much as laughing and making people laugh, he might have won more tournaments. Of course, I wouldn't have liked him as much.

Ben Hogan

Lee Trevino relieves his tensions by talking all the time, to other people, to himself, even sometimes in midswing. Man, how he talks!

Jack Nicklaus

I had trouble breathing, but I was paired with Lee Trevino and he had me laughing all the way around.

Fuzzy Zoeller—about the 1979 Masters, his first, which he won

I loved playing with [Ben] Hogan because I knew he wouldn't say anything to me. That was good, because it helped me concentrate better.

Sam Snead

Arnold [Palmer] is the best I've ever seen at signing autographs, or going out of his way to smile when he's frowning inside.

Peter Jacobsen

He knows how to deal with people. He's probably the greatest people person in the history of golf.

Mark O'Meara—on Arnold Palmer

I used to think Arnold Palmer could walk on water. Now I know it.

Chi Chi Rodriguez—after Palmer made two holes-in-one on the same hole in two days in 1986

Arnold Palmer was my hero. To see him with those late charges, tugging at those pants, that was something.

Raymond Floyd

There never has been a guy who has done as much for sports as Arnie has for golf.

Tom Watson

I think he has more belief in himself, more supreme confidence, than any golfer ever. He thinks he deserves to win and that he's destined to win. So he does win. It's written all over him.

Ben Crenshaw—on Jack Nicklaus

If you couldn't putt, you'd be selling hot dogs out here.

Ben Hogan—to Billy Casper, who one-putted thirty-one of the seventy-two holes in the 1959 U.S. Open

Most successful golfers are loners—they like to golf alone and eat alone.

Bernard Gallagher

You have to be a loner to be successful.

Nancy Lopez

People talk about Tom Watson not having any personality, but he's one hell of a golfer. He's beating all our brains out. If it matters, he's also a nice guy.

Jack Nicklaus

The great players, from [Harry] Vardon to [Jack] Nicklaus, invariably have been great putters.

Tom Watson

If I had to choose one player to hit a life-or-death five-foot putt, it would be Tom Watson in his prime. The guy had absolutely no fear.

Peter Jacobsen

He plays the game of golf as if he has a plane to catch. As if he were double-parked and left the meter running. Guys move slower leaving hotel fires.

Jim Murray—on Corey Pavin

He's like a little dog that gets hold of your pants leg and won't let go.

Mark O'Meara—on Corey Pavin

For a guy who comes wrapped up in such a nice, warm package, he has a fire that could light up a whole city.

Peter Jacobsen—on Paul Azinger

In addition to his qualities as a golfer, Ernie Els is a fine young man, an ideal role model for youngsters, and a person I like immensely.

Gary Player

Faldo doesn't say anything. He doesn't even watch you. He's off in another world.

Brad Bryant—on Nick Faldo as a playing partner

On the course, Scott is so good he's almost—I hate to say it—boring. But later it hits you how awesome he was.

Larry Mize—on Scott Simpson

Seve [Ballesteros] is a genius, one of the few true geniuses in the game. The thing is, Seve is never in trouble. He's in the trees quite a lot, but that's not trouble for him. That's normal.

Ben Crenshaw

We can never quite describe the man he was; we can only try to learn from his example what golf and life are all about.

Ben Crenshaw—on Bobby Jones

Raymond [Floyd is] the most intimidating player I've ever played against. He plays every shot like it's the last shot of his life. He's like a black leopard, stalking the jungle.

Mark O'Meara

[Jack] Nicklaus is able to put himself in an intense frame of mind, where nothing breaks his concentration and he can almost will the ball into the hole.

Ben Crenshaw

A lot of us are good but Jack [Nicklaus] adds one intangible. I think he knows exactly what his capabilities are in any given situation. We may think we can pull off a shot, or even be pretty sure, but Jack knows.

Raymond Floyd

You know he's gonna beat you, he knows he's gonna beat you, and he knows you know he's gonna beat you.

Leonard Thompson—on Jack Nicklaus

He fouled up once. He never got the bar set up in the players' lounge-.

Lee Trevino—kidding Billy Casper after he captained the winning 1979 Ryder Cup team

Sam was born warmed up. If you cut him, 3-in-One oil would come out, not blood.

Gardner Dickinson—on Sam Snead, then 69 years old

Her execution was so great, she was like a machine.

Kathy Whitworth—on Louise Suggs

Of all the players I've watched, men and women, nobody could swing a golf club as well as Mickey Wright. In her overall game, she was just head and shoulders above everyone.

Kathy Whitworth

One of the qualities that separates guys like Seve Ballesteros and Lee Trevino from the rest of the world is an intangible—imagination.

Greg Norman

Greg Norman is good for golf because he plays with such bravado. He's confident and flamboyant, and he hits shots that other players can't hit.

Peter Jacobsen

Seve's a rare kind of guy. He's an excitable golfer who can concentrate.

Larry Nelson—on Seve Ballesteros

To this day, I can think of no player who consistently aligns himself more accurately than [Jack] Nicklaus.

Greg Norman

I haven't seen them all, but I don't know anyone [who] could hit the ball better than Moe Norman.

Lee Trevino

Hubert Green just fidgeted thirty-six times, sneaking a peek at the flag, as he addressed a shot. Hubie's the king of peekers. Someday he's going to be wiggling and waggling, turning his head fifty times as he gets ready to pull the trigger, and he's not going to be able to hit it. He's just going to keep on turning that head until it falls off, or until they send somebody out to bring him in.

Dave Stockton

To me, he's very boring. He's never in the trees or in the water. He's not the best driver, not the best putter. He's just the best at everything.

Fred Couples—on Nick Faldo

[Tom] Kite is one of the best golfers, pound for pound, that ever played the game.

Peter Jacobsen

Isao Aoki may have the best short game in the world, due to a magical touch in his hands and wrists and the fact that he knows how to practice.

Peter Jacobsen

Greg Norman can lead the golf tournament, throw the party that night and entertain everybody till the wee hours, then wake up the next day and beat your brains out.

Peter Jacobsen

When Jack Nicklaus plays well, he wins. When he plays badly, he finishes second. When he plays terribly, he finishes third.

Johnny Miller

Tom Watson's a great golfer, but that's all. Larry Nelson, a nice guy but so absolutely colorless you'd think he'd at least wear some bright clothes. Lon Hinkle, forget it. Ben Crenshaw's Texas drawl is his charisma. Bill Rogers, nothing. Hale Irwin ought to be a banker. Most of the guys don't even drink. Only bullfighting and the waterhole are left as vestigial evidence of what bloody savages men used to be.

Tommy Bolt—on the dullness of the PGA
Tour after Jack Nicklaus's heyday

When Fuzzy [Zoeller] first became known, after he won the Masters, I thought he was funny from trying to be funny. But now I'm convinced it's just natural. He's like Lee Trevino, but Lee's humor is more cutting. Fuzzy is softer. There's a truth in humor and Fuzzy will take it right to the edge of being questionable. Lee sometimes goes over.

Larry Nelson

His driving is unbelievable. I don't go that far on my holidays.

Ian Baker-Finch—on John Daly

I couldn't care less who I'm paired with.

Jack Nicklaus

Freddie [Couples] is the type of player who improves the image of the sport because he's a kind person, has no arrogance, and is totally focused on golf.

Peter Jacobsen

Raymond Floyd is the ultimate bare-knuckle fighter.

David Leadbetter, golf coach

Like a hurricane, his arrival came without warning and his game spells danger wherever he plays.

David Leadbetter—on John Daly

Never before has a player dominated the women's game with such an overwhelming display of power as the self-taught Laura Davies.

David Leadbetter

A smart fella once told me that a fine golfer only has one thing, and that's his fine golf—and that if he forgets it, he's a fool. Tom Watson never forgets.

Byron Nelson

Paul Azinger is a true inspiration to all golfers. He plays with his heart as well as his mind. If Norman Rockwell had painted a family man/golfer, he would have done a portrait of Paul.

Dave Stockton

If this is how he is every week, then it's over. He's the greatest player in the history of the game.

Peter Jacobsen—on Tiger Woods, after he placed fifth, third, first, third, and first in a series of tournaments soon after turning pro

I don't think we've had a whole lot happen in, what, ten years? I mean, some guys here have come on and won a few tournaments, but nobody has sustained and dominated. I think we might have somebody now.

Jack Nicklaus—on Tiger Woods

Competition

Competitive golf is played mainly on a five-and-a half-inch course: the space between your ears.

Bobby Jones

[The exemption] is a blessing and a curse. I would never I give my exemption back, but it made me very complacent. I relaxed for a while. It has happened to a lot of players. All of a sudden, the urgency goes out of your game.

Wayne Grady

If the water is rough in Santander Bay, you fight harder in the boat. You do not give up.

Seve Ballesteros, the son of a fisherman

Raymond has not seen the Taj Mahal, the Great Wall of China—or the last of me.

Payne Stewart—after losing the 1986 U.S. Open to Raymond Floyd

The competitor inside you knows what has to be done. If the game doesn't eat you up inside, you can't possibly be a great player.

Lee Trevino

I turn mean with a six-stroke lead. I'm not happy with a two-shot win. I want more. I want to demoralize them.

Johnny Miller

In competition, I have not regarded seriously the tendency of some people to endow golfers with superhuman powers.

Bobby Jones

How would you like to meet the top 143 people at what you do each week in order to survive?

Bruce Crampton

I love competition so much that when I'm alone, I compete with myself.

Bruce Lietzke

If you have to remind yourself to concentrate during competition, you have no chance to concentrate.

Bobby Nichols

It's fun to see Greg [Norman] winning and enjoying it so much. It's tremendous for golf … You can't help but pat the guy on the back, he's so fresh and honest about it.

Peter Jacobsen

It is not solely the capacity to make great shots that makes champions, but the essential quality of making very few bad shots.

Tommy Armour

I never rooted against an opponent, but I never rooted for him either.

Arnold Palmer

I've had dinner with three players in fourteen years out here. I don't want to get to know these guys. With nine holes to play, I want them to worry about not knowing me.

Lee Trevino

Each time we play, we leave a little piece of ourselves on the course. You never know how much longer you'll be competitive.

Dan Forsman

Confidence

Confidence is everything. From there, it's a small step to winning.

Craig Stadler

Confidence has to be the golfer's greatest single weapon on the green.

Jack Nicklaus

During my winning streaks I got to the point where I thought I was never going to lose. Everything was so automatic and so easy. I was so confident, I felt no one could beat me.

Nancy Lopez

The average golfer has always to fight tension; never may he feel entirely comfortable, or enjoy a complete confidence in his ability to make the shot required.

Bobby Jones

Confidence in golf means being able to concentrate on the problem at hand with no outside interference.

Tom Watson

Most golfers prepare for disaster. A good golfer prepares for success.

Bob Toski

You must always be positive, because your body can only do what your brain sees.

Chi Chi Rodriguez

I'm going to make it.

Tom Watson—to his caddie, before holing a birdie chip called "The shot heard 'round the world" on the 17th at Pebble Beach on the 71st hole at the 1982 U.S. Open. Watson birdied the 18th to win.

It was one of those days you dream about. Every hole seemed to be six inches wide.

Tom Purtzer—after a 66 in the third round of the 1977 L.A. Open

A long drive is good for the ego.

Arnold Palmer

Confidence is the key to putting.

Tony Lema

Golf is a game of days ... and I can beat anyone on my day.

Fuzzy Zoeller

There are times when a golfer must take this game by the scruff of the neck and give it a good, hard shake.

Billy Casper

One thing you don't ever do is think of bad things when you're over a ball. People might think about bad shots, but I don't—even on shots I might be scared to hit.

Fred Couples

Golf is very hard to explain. I could feel it in my hands. I knew I was going to make it ... I just knew.

Greg Norman—on making a forty-four-foot putt for par

If you need a par, go for a birdie, because if you don't get the birdie, you should hopefully get the par.

Nick Faldo

Confidence without ability is impossible to maintain. You can't feel confident very long if you don't know how to hit the ball.

Doug Ford

Once you have the confidence, once your swing and everything have given your mind confidence, then it is all mental. Your mind will automatically tell you, "Do this. Do that."

Nick Faldo

Ball-striking comes from a tremendous amount of confidence. And confidence comes from working extremely hard.

Lee Trevino

You have to train the mind for success. When I first joined the tour, I didn't think I was as good as I was. Now my mental has caught up with my physical.

Calvin Peete

If I ever think anybody is better than me, then I can never be the best. I always have to believe I'm the best.

Payne Stewart

You'll never increase your driving distance without a positive mental attitude. Confidence is vital.

Greg Norman

Be brave, be bold, and take your best shot.

Gay Brewer

Course Observations

A good golf course makes you want to play so badly that you hardly have time to change your shoes.

Ben Crenshaw

Approach the golf course as a friend, not an enemy.

Arnold Palmer

You must play the course within your capabilities.

Julius Boros

There is an ideal route for every golf hole ever built. The more precisely you can identify it, the greater your chances for success.

Jack Nicklaus

I can't swing the way I want to with four sweaters and my pajamas and a rain jacket on.

Lee Trevino—on playing in Scotland

I enjoy golfing in every country, but I must say that the best turf for golf is found in England, where there is so much moisture in the air.

Gary Player

There's more to be learned here about course design than anywhere. Collection bunkers, false fronts, bump shots. The fundamentals of design became fundamentals because of what's here. And it all happened accidentally. Or maybe accidentally on purpose.

Jack Nicklaus—on St. Andrews

The Old Course is a puzzle … and no one's ever going to completely figure it out.

Tom Watson—on St. Andrews

The more I studied the Old Course, the more I loved it, and the more I loved it, the more I studied it.

Bobby Jones—on St. Andrews

I have already said hundreds of times that I like it better than any golf course I have ever played and although I have played it many, many times, its charm for me increases with every round.

Bobby Jones—on St. Andrews

There's nothing wrong with the St. Andrews course that 100 bulldozers couldn't put right. The Old Course needs a dry clean and press.

Ed Furjol

You can play a damned good shot and find the ball in a damned bad place.

George Duncan—on St. Andrews

The reason the Road Hole is the hardest par-4 in the world is because it's a par-5.

Ben Crenshaw—on St. Andrews's 17th hole

How about the 9:40 train out of St. Andrews?

Andrew Kirkaldy—golf pro at the Royal and Ancient Golf Club, when asked (about 14th hole's Hell bunker) "How do I get out of here?"

To me, the ground here is hallowed. The grass grows greener, the trees bloom better, there is even warmth to the rocks ... somehow or other the sun seems to shine brighter on The Country Club than any other place I have known.

Francis Ouimet—on the course at Brookline, Massachusetts

Golf architects should live and play here before they build golf courses.

Tom Watson—on Ballybunion Old Course

One of the scariest opening holes in golf.

Tony Jacklin—on the first hole at Muirfield, Scotland

The people of Royal Melbourne are proud of their greens—they can have them. The greens are the biggest joke since Watergate.

Lee Trevino

Utter predictability in a golf course to me spells blandness, and blandness spells dullness.

Jack Nicklaus

The Augusta National course, where the Masters tournament is held annually, reminds me of a mousetrap with a piece of cheese in the middle. If you get too greedy the trap will crush you.

Gary Player

Of all the courses in the world, Augusta National places the most emphasis on strategy and is the best example of what a major is all about.

David Graham

The course is perfection and it asks for perfection.

Nick Faldo—on Augusta National

It's like a black widow. It seduces you, entices you, romances you—and then it stings you, kills you emotionally.

Mac O'Grady—on Augusta National

Every good course has a couple of holes where everybody talks about the tough decisions to make in club selection. But here [Augusta National], there are thirteen or fourteen holes like that.

John Mahaffey

When you get on this Augusta course, it's a given fact that you're going to get nailed. The variable is how you accept it.

Joe Inman

If there's a golf course in heaven, I hope it's like Augusta National. I just don't want an early tee time.

Gary Player

If I owned a Rembrandt, I don't think I'd want to go slapping on some reds and yellows just because it was kind of dull.

Raymond Floyd—on the "improvements" to Oak Hill

Tell me, do you chaps actually play this hole, or do you just photograph it?

Edward F. Story—former British Walker Cupper
after seeing the scenic first hole at Pine Valley

Ask every professional on tour what his five favorite golf courses are in the world, and the one name that will be on everybody's list is Pebble Beach.

Tom Watson

If I had only one more round of golf to play, I would choose to play it at Pebble Beach.

Jack Nicklaus

If you're 5 over when you hit this tee, it's the best place in the world to commit suicide.

Lee Trevino—on Pebble Beach's 6th hole

Pebble Beach is built right around my game. Unfortunately, it doesn't touch any part of it.

Mason Rudolph

Pebble Beach and Cypress Point make you want to play golf they're such interesting and enjoyable layouts. Spyglass Hill, now that's different; that makes you want to go fishing.

Jack Nicklaus

Robert Trent Jones must have laid out the course in a kennel.

Bob Rosburg—on the Hazeltine National Golf Club (Minnesota), which has ten dogleg holes

Awful, artificial, unfair and ugly.

Tom Watson—on the 17th hole at the Pete Dye–designed PGA West outside Palm Springs, California

You want controversy? Okay, let's have controversy ... A lot of guys would like to put a bomb under that thing.

Jack Nicklaus—on Ponte Vedra

These greens are like used car lots ... It's a chore to play here.

Tom Watson—on Ponte Vedra

When I first look at designing a hole, I consider what Mother Nature has already created on that property, and then I try to mold a golf hole that fits very naturally into what is there ... I guess you could say that Mother Nature is a co-designer of each of my courses.

Jack Nicklaus

What a beautiful place a golf course is. From the meanest country pasture to the Pebble Beaches and St. Andrewses of the world, a golf course is to me a holy ground. I feel God in the trees and grass and flowers, in the rabbits and the birds and squirrels, in the sky and the water. I feel that I am home.

Harvey Penick, golf coach

Failure

Golf is mostly a game about failures.

Tommy Aaron

People are always telling me I should do one thing or another. I should change my grip or shorten my swing. I should practice more and goof around less. I shouldn't smile on Sunday ... I should ... I shouldn't... I should ... I shouldn't. Frankly, I don't know why they worry. It's my life—and I don't worry.

Fred Couples—on criticism of his history of near-misses

One reason golf is such an exasperating game is that a thing we learned is so easily forgotten, and we find ourselves struggling year after year with faults we had discovered and corrected time and again.

Bobby Jones

It's a little odd checking on flights out of town on Friday.

56-year-old Joanne Carner—after missing the cut at the 1995 U.S. Women's Open, for the first time in twenty-six years

I hit it perfectly, but it wouldn't go in.

Tom Kite—after missing a putt on the 72nd hole at the Masters that would have taken winner Jack Nicklaus into a playoff

The toughest thing for most people to learn in golf is to accept bad holes— and then forget about them.

Gary Player

I was so apprehensive. I got so many over par and felt the whole of Australia had sat up all night watching me screw up. I believed I had failed. But after about a week I realized that just because you fail, it doesn't make you a failure.

Ian Baker-Finch—after his fourth-round 79 in the 1984 British Open (he had led after three rounds)

I hate a hook. It nauseates me. I could vomit ... it's like a rattlesnake in your pocket.

Ben Hogan

I don't get morose about it, because there is no point. I'll go home, down a few beers, and that is that.

Greg Norman

I go anywhere, they know me. I go to Japan, they know me! I never see a player miss a putt and become so famous. I just miss a putt. I don't kill anybody.

Costantino Rocca—reflecting on his miss of a four-foot putt on the 17th hole of the final round of the '93 Ryder Cup, which allowed the Americans to win on the 18th

I played poorly for so long that I lost all confidence. I found out it takes a long time to overcome all the negative thoughts.

Bob Tway

Like most professional golfers, I have a tendency to remember my poor shots a shade more vividly than the good ones.

Ben Hogan

I'm a mental basket case. I have the mind of a 12-year-old, a total waste of space.

Mark Calcavecchia—following a disappointing showing at the Colonial

Even if you hit forty bad shots, you should still keep trying. The other fellow might have hit forty-one.

Gary Player

The key to success on the tour—or at any level of play, for that matter—is not letting the down period get to you and make your game worse than it is. You just have to be patient and work your way out of it.

Al Geiberger

The game just embarrasses you until you feel inadequate and pathetic. You want to cry like a child.

Craig Stadler

When the tournament player misses a short putt, almost every spectator says to himself, "What a dog he is; I could have made that one myself easily."

Tommy Armour

The first thing I do after losing, regardless of whether I lost a close one because of a silly lapse or simply was snowed under by a rival running on a hot streak, is to forget it. I take a look at my calendar and start thinking about where we'll be playing next week, and I'll show 'em then!

Nancy Lopez

Only about fifty or sixty times a day.

Tom Kite—on being asked if he still thought
about a heartbreaking loss in the 1989 U.S. Open

I suddenly realized who I was and where I was.

Johnny Miller—on being asked what happened
when he bogeyed twice at the 1971 Masters, missing a playoff

It's terrifying to think of all the gremlins that can creep into your game. Our margin for error is infinitesimal.

Roger Maltbie

If you hit a bad shot, just tell yourself it is great to be alive, relaxing and walking around on a beautiful golf course. The next shot will be better.

Al Geiberger

When you miss a shot, never think of what you did wrong. Come up to the next shot thinking of what you must do right.

Tommy Armour

There is nothing so demoralizing as missing a short putt.

Bobby Jones

The better I have become, the more I have embarrassed myself by my failures; and the more I have embarrassed myself, the more I have been goaded into trying to develop greater skills.

Jack Nicklaus

If I'd won, it woulda been some story, wouldn't it? But if I'd won, nobody would have seen the sensitive side [of me].

Curtis Strange—after an emotional reaction to
losing the 1985 Masters despite a dramatic comeback

You know you can't hide. It's like you're walking down the fairway naked. The gallery knows what you've done, every other player knows and, worst of all, you know. That's when you find out if you're a competitor.

Hale Irwin

I'm sick of playing lousy … First it irritates you, then it really bothers you, until finally you get so damn blasted mad at yourself that you decide to do something about it. I've decided to do something. And I will.

Jack Nicklaus

Do not be ashamed of choking … any golfer who has never choked on the golf course should be in an asylum … Sooner or later all normal human beings encounter situations on the course that they are not, at that particular moment, emotionally capable of handling.

Paul Runyan

When you struggle with the putter, it gets to the rest of your game. It's an extra strain on yourself to try to squeeze that ball in the hole.

Ben Crenshaw

The traditions of the game are rich with memories of dramatic triumphs as well as heartbreaking failures. The best players fail the most because they are in the hunt all the time. You learn to handle it—accept it or you don't survive.

Deane Beman

When the great player screws up, he says, "I'm going to work on that and not do it again." The bad player says, "Boy, I screwed up again. I guess I really am a dog."

Peter Jacobsen

I hate to lose. But in golf, everybody loses because it is so hard mentally.

Tiger Woods

Love and Marriage

Golf is like a love affair. If you don't take it seriously, it's no fun; if you do take it seriously, it breaks your heart.

Arnold Daly

When I come back in the next life, I want to come back as a golf pro's wife. She wakes up every morning at the crack of ten and is faced by her first major decision of the day: whether to have breakfast in bed or in the hotel coffee shop.

Don Sikes

My wife doesn't care what I do when I'm away as long as I don't have a good time.

Lee Trevino

The only thing I ever asked of Joan was that if she was angry with me, please don't say anything until after my round. The game was difficult enough without trying to play after arguing with my wife.

Paul Runyan

Time does not pass when I am gone from you.

Costantino Rocca—in a note to his wife, Antonella

We were happily married for eight months. Unfortunately, we were married for four and a half years.

Nick Faldo

She knows how to hang on to her money. I wish her mom were the same way.

Orville Moody—on his caddie/daughter

What you have when you play twenty Senior events and make about fifteen regular tour stops is divorce.

Miller Barber

She'll just tell me, "Stop acting like a big jerk." She really puts the hammer down and sets me straight. Like when I miss a three-footer, and all I can think is "It's not my fault!" I used to be good at that.

Mark Calcavecchia—about his wife, Sheryl Timms

Countless marriages, friendships, and business relationships have been destroyed by the game, directly or indirectly.

Larry Miller

There's something else to live for, something else to come home to. I've got a wife, a son, and a daughter and they are so much more important to me than golf.

Nick Price

Women golfers are wonderful. The men may not agree with me on this score, but when it comes to women golfers I know whereof I speak. I married one.

Gary Player

My wife always said she wanted to marry a millionaire. Well, she married a millionaire. I used to be a multimillionaire.

Lee Trevino

Before I was married, I used to love being alone in a hotel room on the tour, where I don't even have to make my bed, let alone ever cook anything or clean up. Now I feel lonely out there.

Nancy Lopez

The worst thing about being a professional golfer is the time you're away from home.

Bruce Lietzke

I just thought about how much I loved her. There was nothing else like it. To have a wife like I have, to be able to share that moment with her.

Lee Janzen—on why he embraced his wife just after winning the 1993 U.S. Open

How can they beat me? I've been struck by lightning, had two back operations, and been divorced twice.

Lee Trevino

I tell you, I love my wife probably more'n golf.

John Daly—who has been married three times, so far

The Inner Game

I'm about five inches from being an outstanding golfer. That's the distance my left ear is from my right.

Ben Crenshaw

Thinking instead of acting is the number one golf disease.

Sam Snead

You must attain a neurological and biological serenity in chaos. You cannot let yourself be sabotaged by adrenaline.

Mac O'Grady

The mind messes up more shots than the body.

Tommy Bolt

He [the golfer] must have the courage to keep trying in the face of ill luck or disappointment, and timidity to appreciate and appraise the dangers of each stroke, and to curb the desire to take chances beyond reasonable hope of success.

Bobby Jones

The whole secret of mastering the game of golf—and this applies to the beginner as well as to the pro—is to cultivate a mental approach to the game that will enable you to shrug off the bad shots, shrug off the bad days, keep patient and know in your heart that sooner or later you will be back on top.

Arnold Palmer

Golf is a difficult game, but it's a little easier if you trust your instincts. It's too hard a game to try to play like someone else.

Nancy Lopez

Golf is a spiritual game. It's like Zen. You have to let your mind take over.

Amy Alcott

The moment I hit it, I felt something in my bones.

Gene Sarazen—on his double eagle at the 1935 Masters

When I'm in a zone, I don't think about the shot or the wind or the distance or the gallery or anything; I just pull a club and swing.

Mark Calcavecchia

A bad attitude is worse than a bad swing.

Payne Stewart

Of all the hazards, fear is the worst.

Sam Snead

The human mind is the most powerful thing in this world and scientists say we only use 10 percent of it. Well, I'm sure that's certain in golf. You've got more electrical connections in your head than a whole city. You'll do anything to keep 'em from going blooey on you in the crunch.

Joe Inman

When I'm in this state, everything is pure, vividly clear. I'm in a cocoon of concentration.

Tony Jacklin

Be patient. Acquiring finesse takes time.

Amy Alcott

You can't do it unless you've imagined it first.

Peter Jacobsen—on six-foot putting

It is the complaint of all golfers that on some days they have the feel and on others the magic touch entirely deserts them.

Bobby Jones

A great round of golf is a lot like a terrible round. You drift into a zone, and it is hard to break out of it.

Al Geiberger

Your final goal is to convert your athletic swing to pure instinct rather than conscious thought.

David Leadbetter

The pro—watch him next time—is always thinking.

Arnold Palmer

Trust your "muscle memory" to take over.

Ernie Els

Anger has no place on the course.

Sandra Palmer

The mental attitude in which we approach a short putt has a lot to do with our success.

Bobby Jones

Out on the golf course factors such as wind speed, pin position, distance to the flag, and any hazards can play havoc with your decision making.

Ernie Els

I didn't play my best golf, but I kept focused better than I ever had. I stayed in the present tense all week.

Tom Kite—after winning the 1992 U.S. Open

You can win tournaments when you're mechanical, but golf is a game of emotion and adjustment. If you're not aware of what's happening to your mind and your body when you're playing, you'll never be able to be the very best you can be.

Jack Nicklaus

Be decisive. A wrong decision is generally less disastrous than indecision.

Bernhard Langer

You can talk about strategy all you want, but what really matters is resiliency.

Hale Irwin

A strong mind is one of the key components that separates the great from the good.

Gary Player

The zone is the ability to give 110 percent of your attention and your focus to the shot. When I'm on the tee, I'll see a divot in the fairway and try to run my ball over that divot—and succeed. That's the zone.

Nick Price

I practice visualization. The clearer you can visualize the shot, the greater chance your body has of producing it. If you don't have a real clear picture before you hit, the shot will come up fuzzy.

Brad Bryant

All of us have an "inner clock," a certain pace at which we function most comfortably and effectively.

Ken Venturi

Inspiration

I'm in love with golf and I want everybody else to share my love affair.

Arnold Palmer

If the sun is up, why aren't you playing golf?

Lee Trevino

I owe a lot to golf. It's a debt I'll never be able to repay.

Gary Player

Home, home on the range ...

Tom Watson

The game has such a hold on golfers because they compete not only against an opponent, but also against the course, against par, and most surely—against themselves.

Gary Player

Second doesn't matter. Second is about as important as fifty-second. Winning is the reason you are playing.

Arnold Palmer

A good swing is a physical pleasure.

Ben Hogan

When I play my best golf, I feel as if I'm in a fog, standing back watching the earth in orbit with a golf club in my hands.

Mickey Wright

I've never shortchanged myself on dreams.

Tom Kite

Your frame of reference must be exactly the width of the cup, not the general vicinity. When you're putting well, the only question is what part of the hole it's going to fall in, not if it's going in.

Jack Nicklaus

I'm constantly looking at my grip, posture, and aim. Golf is my living and I can't afford to take anything for granted.

Ernie Els

One of the greatest pleasures in golf—I can think of nothing that truly compares with it unless it is watching a well-played shot streak for the flag—is the sensation a golfer experiences at the instant he contacts the ball flush and correctly.

Ben Hogan

What's classic? Beethoven's Fifth? The Mona Lisa? Michelangelo's David? My definition of "classic" is the following: any creation which stands up to the test of time because it does not deviate from the standards of perfection for a particular art form. Classic golf swings are rare.

Patty Sheehan

Keep your sense of humor. There's enough stress in the rest of your life to let bad shots ruin a game you're supposed to enjoy.

Amy Alcott

I'm a golfer. I like to win. I'm not afraid to dicker with any part of my game at any time. I'm a fiddler. I enjoy working at the things that let you win.

Jack Nicklaus

To play well on the final holes of a major championship, you need a certain arrogance. You have to find a trance, some kind of self-hypnosis that's almost a state of grace.

Hale Irwin

What does it take to be a champion? Desire, dedication, determination, concentration, and the will to win.

Patty Berg

People tell me, "Jim, now you got it made." I know better. I know where I'm from. Now I got to work three times as hard to stay where I am.

Jim Thorpe

I guess the allure of golf is really the next shot ... always trying to hit it perfectly, to get that feeling.

Curtis Strange

When one thing is working, it helps the next thing. You just go from strength to strength.

Greg Norman

All golfers, men and women, professional and amateur, are united by one thing: their desire to improve.

Judy Rankin

Desire is the bottom line. You've got to have 100 percent desire. Anything less is complacency.

Tom Watson

It's just one of those days when you hit what I would consider perfect putts. I hit edge after edge after edge.

Tiger Woods

That walk was the warmest feeling and the coldest streak down my back of my life.
Fuzzy Zoeller—about his walk up the 18th fairway
en route to winning the 1984 U.S. Open

You can get caught up in being too nice and just playing along. You have days when you need to turn it on.

Nick Faldo

Hit fairways, hit greens, sink putts.

Ernie Els

Hey, let's go party!
Mark Calcavecchia—on being asked what he wanted to do after a
heartbreaking loss to Sandy Lyle in the 1988 Masters

The Majors

No matter what a player does the rest of his playing days, he will be most remembered for winning major titles.

Peter Jacobsen

Just to play in it is great. To do well in it is fantastic. To win it is a dream.
Ian Baker-Finch—after winning the 1991 British Open

This is the real World Series of Golf.

Tom Watson—on the British Open

It's sort of a war out there. There's a mental discipline involved unlike at regular tour events, where the guys think they are entitled to make a birdie all the time.

Hale Irwin—on the U.S. Open

I've been nervous all week. Now I'm just bloody terrified.
Tony Jacklin—before the final round of the 1969 British Open—which he won

Winning in Scotland beats winning anywhere else. I'm a traditionalist and a sentimentalist and there's nothing like winning a championship in the birthplace of golf. This tournament is what golf is all about. You cannot love golf any more than you do when you come down the 18th fairway of this golf course a champion.

Tom Watson—after winning the British Open for the third time (at Muirfield, 1980)

The British Open is my favorite [tournament] by far. I enjoy playing in terrible conditions. It's like playing in North Texas and Oklahoma, where I grew up. I like the people. It's the purest classic golf tournament. And the beer is good in Scotland too.

Andrew Magee

The first time I played the Masters, I was so nervous I drank a bottle of rum before I teed off. I shot the happiest 83 of my life.

Chi Chi Rodriguez

The final round of the [U.S.] Open is not so much a test of golf as a test of judgment.

Jack Nicklaus

Playing in the U.S. Open is like tippy-toeing through hell.

Jerry McGee

The Masters is a perfect example of how the pressure of golf—and the buildup about how important it is—can change you so that you hardly know yourself.

Joe Inman.

I get too jazzed up. The first round has killed me for fifteen straight years.

Johnny Miller—on the Masters

If they renamed it the Hartford Open, everyone would shoot 265. Take away the pressure and all these young bucks would shoot the lights out.

Lee Trevino—on the Masters

Somewhere in those first one to four weeks that followed [a playoff win in the Masters], it hit me. I can't remember the exact moment, but I'm sure, when I was layin' in bed, I thought, "My God, I did win that sucker."

Craig Stadler

I've never been to heaven and, thinkin' back on my life, I probably won't get a chance to go. I guess the Masters is as close as I'm going to get.

Fuzzy Zoeller—winner of the 1979 Masters

When you lose a major, it's like a death in the family.

Ken Venturi

Unfortunately, when you're assessed at the end of your career, it's majors that count, not money in the bank.

Tom Kite

Media Matters

I once thought of becoming a political cartoonist because they only have to come up with one idea a day. Then I thought I'd become a sportswriter instead, because they don't have to come up with any.

Sam Snead

I like the pressroom because you can always get something good to eat and drink.

Rocky Thompson

They need to look at their own lives before they use that pen. I'm sure a lot of those guys in the media don't have perfect lives.

John Daly

A good rule of thumb for broadcasters is the same one often used by players: you better bring your game to the golf course, because you can't count on finding it once you get there.

Peter Jacobsen

I don't know ... if I did, I might have won this tournament.
*Tom Weiskopf—on being asked what was going
through Jack Nicklaus's mind at a Masters he ended up winning*

I was afraid to move my lips in front of the TV cameras. The commissioner probably would have fined me just for what I was thinking.
Tom Weiskopf—on bad shots in the 1980 Masters

I'm always afraid there might be somebody at the other end.
*Fred Couples—on not answering the
phone after his string of victories in 1991 and 1992*

We have almost no controversy. Maybe I should get in a fistfight with Jack Nicklaus on the 18th green.
Tom Watson—on golf's modest TV ratings

… an affliction known as rabbit ears. It's caused by letting people's off-the-cuff comments slip through your auditory canal and into your brain. It's especially prevalent with golf broadcasters.

Peter Jacobsen

Golf is a nice game, but that's it. It's never been an exciting game to watch on TV. It's not a circus and never will be one.

Jack Nicklaus

I'd like to thank the media from the heart of my bottom.

Nick Faldo

Mentors

Tutorage under a competent instructor is worth much more than the slight remuneration you will pay him.

Sam Snead

Don't be too proud to take lessons. I'm not.

Jack Nicklaus

No one becomes a champion without help.

Johnny Miller

The professional, aside from being your teacher, has your interests at heart … He will listen to your lamentations—why the putt didn't drop on the 18th, or why you hooked in the rough on the 11th. He will be your father confessor of golf. Take your golf troubles to him.

Sam Snead

There has been criticism that some professional golfers do not know how to teach. In defense of my competent colleagues in professional golf, I must point out that many pupils don't know how to take a lesson.

Tommy Armour

The practice ground is an evil place. It's full of so-called coaches waiting to pounce. You can see them waiting to dish their mumbo-jumbo. To hell with coaches.

Ernie Els

I've never had a coach in my life. When I find one who can beat me, then I'll listen.

Lee Trevino

Rhythm and timing we all must have, yet no one knows how to teach either.

Bobby Jones

He persuaded rather than pushed me at golf. He always told me not to be afraid if I was behind in a tournament, that I could go out and shoot another good round. If I blew a hole he would tell me to forget it and go on to the next one, I couldn't bring it back.

Nancy Lopez—on her father, Domingo

It is only when he has watched long enough and hard enough to get to the root cause of a problem that he will proffer an opinion.

Jack Nicklaus—on his former coach, Jack Grout

I think I've got a lot of ability to play golf. Couple that with a lot of hard practice, and a good teacher like Peter Kostis, and that's why I got better so fast.

Mark Calcavecchia

The biggest thing he did for me—the key to my success—was to get me to try to hole every shot, to try to focus wholly on knocking every shot into the cup from the fairway.

Ian Baker-Finch—on sports psychologist Bob Rotella

Money Matters

The dollars aren't so important—once you have them.

Johnny Miller

I never wanted to be a millionaire. I just wanted to live like one.

Walter Hagen

I'm third in earnings and first in spending.

Tony Lema

Walter Hagen was the first player I knew that earned one million from golf, and of course he spent it, too. Sam [Snead] earned one million, too—and saved two million.

Fred Corcoran

I'm working as hard as I can to get my life and my cash to run out at the same time. If I can just die after lunch Tuesday, everything will be perfect.

Doug Sanders

Guarantee me three million a year and you can scream, yell, or spit on my ball when I'm putting. Because even if I miss it, I still get paid.

Lee Trevino—on the guaranteed contracts of
baseball and football players

If you expect a miracle, you should expect to pay for one.

Derek Hardy—teaching pro, on why he charges 140 dollars for a series
of thirteen lessons but demands 1,000 dollars for a single session

We had so little to eat that when Mom would throw a bone to the dog, he'd have to call for a fair catch.

Lee Trevino

There's so much money to be made today in Monday events and at foreign tournaments that it's hard for anyone to dominate. It's a lot harder to concentrate on big events when you have so many lucrative distractions.

Jack Nicklaus

You drive for show and putt for dough.

Bobby Locke

In a major championship, you don't care about the money. You're just trying to get your name on a piece of silver.

Nick Faldo

The name of the game is to get the ball in the hole and pick up the check. It's a nice feeling.

Sam Snead

I like the idea of playing for money instead of silverware. I never did like to polish.

Patty Sheehan

I cannot find a job that pays me 700,000 dollars a year, so until I do, I'll be right here.

Pat Bradley

Because we dress well on the course, people think we're all millionaires. The truth is that there is less money in pro golf than in any well-known sport. Out of the 144 guys here, at least 100 are extremely concerned about their next check.

Ed Sneed

A glittering amateur career doesn't always convert into pound signs when you turn pro.

Ernie Els

I owe everything to golf. Where else could a guy with an IQ like mine make this much money?

Hubert Green

The gravy may still keep coming for a while after your game's gone bad, but it disappears pretty fast once people catch on.

John Mahaffey

If you want it, get it and spend it. It's only money, not something to worship. If you run out, go out and get some more.

Mark Calcavecchia

The Nature of the Game

If there is one thing I have learned during my years as a professional, it is that the only thing constant about golf is its inconstancy.

Jack Nicklaus

There is nothing occult about hitting a golf ball.

Bobby Jones

Golf is a game you never can get too good in. You can improve, but you never can get to where you master the game.

Gay Brewer

This is a game of misses. The guy who misses the best is going to win.

Ben Hogan

Golf takes more mental energy, more concentration, more determination than any other sport ever invented.

Arnold Palmer

Golf is a puzzle without an answer.

Gary Player

Anyone who hopes to reduce putting—or any other department of the game for that matter—to an exact science is in for a serious disappointment and will only suffer from the attempt.

Bobby Jones

Golf puts a man's character on the anvil and his richest qualities—patience, poise, and restraint—to the flame.

Billy Casper

The personality of golf is good golf. If you want to see a comedian, you ought to tune in [to] *Saturday Night Live*.

Tom Watson

All golf is divided into three parts: the strokes, the course, and the opponent.

Tommy Armour

What you have got to remember is that it is the panic rather than the one miscreant shot which will make the difference between a good round and bad.

Laura Davies

By and large, your golf game mirrors your personality.

Lanny Wadkins

Baseball may be a game of inches, as they say, but golf is a game of millimeters.

Arnold Palmer

This game is like a horse ... if you take your eye off it, it'll jump back and kick your shins for you.

Byron Nelson

Golf is not a funeral, though both can be very sad affairs.

Bernard Darwin

When you play for fun, it's fun. But when you play golf for a living, it's a game of sorrows. You're never happy.

Gary Player

In golf, when we hit a foul ball, we got to go out and play it.

Sam Snead—comparing golf and baseball

Putting is really a game within a game.

Tom Watson

I have always thought of golf as the best of all games—the most interesting, the most demanding, the most rewarding.

Ben Hogan

I have found the game to be, in all factualness, a universal language wherever I traveled at home or abroad.

Ben Hogan

There is no need to tell one who has played a great deal of championship golf that it's the short game that decides the contests.

Tommy Armour

There are no absolutes in golf. Golf is such an individual game, and no two people swing alike.

Kathy Whitworth

Golf is the one game I know which becomes more and more difficult the longer one plays it.

Bobby Jones

Golf is just a game, and an idiotic one at that.

Mark Calcavecchia—on failing to make the cut at a British Open

Golf is a game where guts, stick-to-it-ness, and blind devotion will get you nothing but an ulcer.

Tommy Bolt

Golf is a game of endless predicaments.

Chi Chi Rodriguez

No one ever conquers golf.

Kathy Whitworth

The vagaries of golf are never more frequently or curiously displayed than they are on the putting green.

Tommy Armour

I've been around this game long enough to know it can leave you just as quickly as it comes to you.

Raymond Floyd

Golf is the "only-est" sport. You're completely alone with every conceivable opportunity to defeat yourself. Golf brings out your assets and liabilities as a person. The longer you play, the more certain you are that a man's perform-ance is the outward manifestation of who, in his heart, he really thinks he is.

Hale Irwin

I'd say our game is about as close to the American Dream as you can get. The harder you work, the more respect you get. Desire means everything out here. Isn't that what our economic and political system is all about? Individual initiative?

John Mahaffey

Guys in other sports, everything is taken care of for them. You could play a whole career in the NFL or NBA and still be a baby. To stay out here, you have to be an adult.

Jim Thorpe

I've heard guys say they wouldn't want golf to be that important to them. Well, it is that important to me and I'm not going to sit here and BS you and tell you it's not. It's my livelihood and my passion.

Curtis Strange

Golf is not a fair game. It's a rude game.

Fuzzy Zoeller

Golf is a game in which perfection stays just out of reach.

Betsy Rawls

An inherent part of the game is a set of virtues that mirrors all the qualities desir-able in society: integrity, honor, respect, rules, and discipline, to name a few.

Larry Miller

Putting is a very personal affair.

Greg Norman

It [golf] is visual, it has texture, it has emotion, it has power.

Betty Jameson

You know, golfers' results are like mirror images of themselves. You just feel like it's your whole life out there.

Ben Crenshaw

The only activities in the world you can enjoy without being any good at are golf and sex.

Jimmy Demaret

Golf is deceptively simple and endlessly complicated. A child can play it well and a grown man can never master it. Any single round of it is full of unexpected triumphs and perfect shots that end in disaster. It is almost a science, yet it is a puzzle without an answer. It is gratifying and tantalizing, precise and unpredictable; it requires complete concentration and total relaxation. It satisfies the soul and frustrates the intellect. It is at the same time rewarding and maddening—and it is without doubt the greatest game mankind has ever invented.

Arnold Palmer

Golf giveth and golf taketh away. But it taketh away a hell of a lot more than it giveth.

Simon Hobday

There are two distinct kinds of golf—just plain golf and tournament golf. Golf—the plain variety—is the most delightful of games, an enjoyable, companionable pastime; tournament golf is thrilling, heartbreaking, terribly hard work—a lot of fun when you are young with nothing much on your mind, but fiercely punishing in the end.

Bobby Jones

Philosophy

I know that I have had greater satisfaction than anyone who ever lived out of the hitting of golf shots.

Ben Hogan

Don't hurry. Don't worry. You're only here on a short visit, so don't forget to stop and smell the flowers.

Walter Hagen

One of the most fascinating things about golf is how it reflects the cycle of life. No matter what you shoot, the next day you have to go back to the first tee and begin all over again and make yourself into something.

Peter Jacobsen

My father say to me, "Respect everybody, and your life, it will be perfect." Then, even if you are poor on the outside, on the inside you are rich.

Costantino Rocca

Pain and suffering are inevitable in our lives, but misery is an option.

Chip Beck

Show me a good loser and I'll show you a seldom winner.

Sam Snead

If just some of the sensible principles that keep players out of trouble in their day-to-day affairs were applied to their golf game, their handicaps would drop drastically.

Greg Norman

What other people may find in poetry or in art museums, I find in the flight of a good drive—the white ball sailing up and up into that blue sky, growing smaller and smaller, almost taking off in orbit, then suddenly reaching its apex, curving downward, falling, describing the perfect parabola of a good hit, and finally dropping to the turf to roll some more, the way I planned it.

Arnold Palmer

You are what you think you are—in golf and in life.

Raymond Floyd

My secret is smoke six or seven cigars, enjoy a little wine at night, have a beautiful wife who loves you, and have a great caddie like mine, that's all.

Larry Laoretti

You hear that winning breeds winning. But no—winners are bred from losing. They learn that they don't like it.

Tom Watson

I had climbed the mountain I'd always dreamed of climbing—and I wanted to rest and enjoy it.

Johnny Miller—on being asked why his game had declined

Love and putting are mysteries for the philosopher to solve. Both subjects are beyond golfers.

Tommy Armour

Spirit-golfers don't play the golf course—the golf course plays them.

Larry Miller

I realize that there are no guarantees in this game—not to mention in this life—and we have only a short time to enjoy it.

Scott Simpson

I like to expect the unexpected.

Greg Norman

My philosophy has always been "What difference does it make?" If you play every week, you're going to have bad days, too. I think that's why I have the reputation of playing well under pressure.

Raymond Floyd

The perfect round of golf has never been played. It's eighteen holes-in-one. I almost dreamt it once, but I lipped out at 18. I was mad as hell.

Ben Hogan

Philosophy

In golf, as in life, you get out of it what you put into it.

Sam Snead

When it comes to the game of life, I figure I've played the whole course.

Lee Trevino

Remember, we play the ball as it lies.

Bobby Jones—on the paralysis that finally took his life

Nothing is ever going to be perfect in this life. You have to expect a little detour now and then.

Greg Norman

One of the best lessons in golf is take what you can get.

Jim Litke

I'm not going to change my life for anybody. I just want to be the best and do it in my own little way. Drink a few beers and have fun.

Ian Woosnam

I realized I came into this world with nothing, and I could leave it with nothing.

Paul Azinger—on being diagnosed with cancer

I had a lot of fun playing golf and met a lot of people. I met kings and queens. Golf has always been good to me, and I hope I did a little to help golf.

Walter Hagen

Honey, I ain't gonna die.

Babe Didrikson Zaharias—her final words spoken to her husband, George Zaharias, from a hospital bed

Practice

Like Gary Player, he just loves to practice. I know because I've played him all around the world. He'll tee it up anywhere there's a golf course and you've got to like a chap like that.

Lee Trevino—on Bernhard Langer

The harder I practice the luckier I get.

Gary Player

You must work very hard to become a natural golfer.

Gary Player

Practice sometimes leads to fiddling and experimenting—and that can be damaging.

Ian Woosnam

It's good to practice at night. You hit the ball and listen. If you hear crack-crack-crack, you know you have hit the trees. Lost ball. But you hear nothing, you know you are in the middle of the fairway.

Costantino Rocca

Practice puts your brains in your muscles.

Sam Snead

The "click" of a solid wood shot soaring far down the fairway is well worth all the hours of practice.

Jimmy Demaret

I never hit a shot, even in practice, without having a very sharp, in-focus picture of it in my head. It's like a color movie.

Jack Nicklaus

There is nothing in this game of golf that can't be improved upon—if you practice.

Patty Berg

Undirected practice is worse than no practice. Too often you become careless and sloppy in your swing. You'd be better off staying home and beating the rugs.

Gary Player

Every day you don't hit balls is one day longer it takes you to get better.

Ben Hogan

We work on putting as much as we do the full swing—after all, if putting is half the game, it deserves half your practice time.

Tom Watson

Don't be too anxious to see good results on the scoreboard until you've fully absorbed the principles of the golf swing on the practice tee.

Louise Suggs

You need a purpose in mind when you practice.

David Leadbetter

I still practice every day when it rains in Spain. That is when I am most comfortable. Everything is empty.

Seve Ballesteros

At some point you say to yourself, "I want to be the best." But when you honestly make that commitment, you have to realize all the dedication and time that it takes.

Raymond Floyd

Practice must be interesting, even absorbing, if it is to be of any use.

Bobby Jones

Practice, which some regard as a chore, should be approached as just about the most pleasant recreation ever devised.

Babe Didrikson Zaharias

Practice until you don't have to think.

Calvin Peete

Pressure and Nerves

We all choke. You just try to choke last.

Tom Watson

That's a bag full of indecision.

Jack Burke—on hearing that Arnold Palmer
brought eight putters to a tournament

I get over the ball and I can't bring myself to pull the putter back. I say to myself, "Hit it, Ben," but the putter just won't move.

Ben Hogan

Putting affects the nerves more than anything else. I would actually get nauseated over three-footers, and there were tournaments when I couldn't get a meal down for four days.

Byron Nelson

That ball sits there and says, "Now idiot, don't hit me in the hazard. Don't hit me over there, hit me on the green. You think you can, idiot? I doubt if you can. Especially when you're choking your guts out."

Davis Love III

My hands were shaking ... the only problem with that is you never know which shake is going to hit the putt.

Patty Sheehan

[Golf is] a compromise between what your ego wants you to do, what experience tells you to do, and what your nerves let you do.

Bruce Crampton

The person I fear most in the last two rounds is myself.

Tom Watson

There were a lot of times when I could have won but didn't. But I persevered and eventually I learned that you don't have to hit the ball perfectly to win; you have to manage yourself better.

Tom Watson

I shot a wild elephant in Africa thirty yards from me, and it didn't hit the ground until it was right at my feet. I wasn't a bit scared. But a four-foot putt scares me to death.

Sam Snead

We all choke, and the man who says he doesn't choke is lying like hell.

Lee Trevino

I'm very tightly wound. All that jabbering is a pressure valve. I couldn't do without it.

Lee Trevino

Fear ruins more golf shots, for duffer and star, than any other one factor.

Tommy Armour

A tense mind breeds tense muscles, and tense muscles make you feel clumsy, out of gear.

Jack Nicklaus

He started to panic as I began creeping up on him. You could see it and feel it.

Billy Casper—on Arnold Palmer during the 1966 U.S. Open playoff

Just because you're nervous doesn't mean you can't hit great shots.

Paul Azinger

These are the hazards of golf: the unpredictability of your own body chemistry, the rub of the green on the courses, the wind and the weather, the bee that lands on your ball or on the back of your neck while you are putting, the sudden noise while you are swinging, the whole problem of playing the game at high mental tension and low physical tension.

Arnold Palmer

Pressure is playing for ten dollars when you don't have a dime in your pocket.

Lee Trevino

Some guys get so nervous playing for their own money, the greens don't need fertilizing for a year.

Dave Hill

Swing tempo has been the most important factor in my career. It relieves the pressure and stress of the game.

Nick Faldo

That ghastly time when, with the first movement of the putter, the golfer blacks out, loses sight of the ball and hasn't the remotest idea of what to do with the putter, or, occasionally, that he is holding a putter at all.

Tommy Armour—defining the "yips"

Yips don't seize the victim during a practice round. It is a tournament disease.

Tommy Armour

The number one source of pressure and choking is that you don't want to let your teammates down. It's the only time all year when you care more about others than yourself. It evokes strange responses in people. Playing for your country is big. But not wanting to let down your peers is bigger.

Johnny Miller—on the Ryder Cup

To control your mind and body throughout a round of golf, with all its pressures and frustrations, is probably the single biggest challenge in golf.

Greg Norman

I do some form of breathing exercises during a pressure situation. It definitely helps. Every time, before I hit a key shot, I take a deep breath and cleanse the mind.

Paul Azinger

Once he started to get the yippies, you could tell right away he was struggling. He'd smoke a whole cigarette before he could bring himself to try and putt.

Sam Snead—on Ben Hogan

I get nervous. I might not show it, but I do. What people see, I guess, is that I'm a slow swinger and I walk slow, and people think that means I'm lackadaisical.

Fred Couples

Preparation is the key to lessening the pressure. Most things that need to be done to reduce pressure should be done prior to the tournament. It's basic stuff like knowing beforehand exactly where you want to hit the ball and how to play each shot.

Bill Murchison

My butterflies are still going strong. I just hope they are flying in formation.

Larry Mize

Do you want to know the definition of scary? Scary is standing in the middle of the fairway with a 7 iron in your hand and having no idea whether you can hit the green or what the shot is going to do. That's scary.

Mark O'Meara

Addressing a golf ball would seem to be a simple matter—that is, to the uninitiated, who cannot appreciate that a golf ball can hold more terrors than a spacious auditorium packed with people.

Bobby Jones

The pressure gets worse the older you get. The hole starts to look the size of a Bayer aspirin.

Gary Player

Reality

There are no secrets—no magic formula.

Ernie Els

They say golf is like life, but don't believe them. Golf is more complicated than that.

Gardner Dickinson

Never bet with anyone you meet on the first tee who has a deep suntan, a 1 iron in his bag, and squinty eyes.

Dave Marr

I don't say my golf game is bad, but if I grew tomatoes they'd come up sliced.

Miller Barber

If he had to play my tee ball all his life, he'd be a pharmacist.

Lee Trevino—comparing his game to that of Jack Nicklaus

Seve Ballesteros and Greg Norman are the superstars. I shall be back washing the dishes tonight at the home we have rented.

Sandy Lyle—answering a question about how it felt to be a superstar

When I was in college, I thought about becoming an attorney. But I wasn't smart enough, I hate being cooped up indoors, and I'm too nice a guy.

Arnold Palmer

I could have played safe, but that wouldn't have been me.

Arnold Palmer—on losing the U.S. Open to Billy Casper

It is nothing new or original to say that golf is played one stroke at a time. But it took me many years to realize it.

Bobby Jones

Reality

What you have to do is shoot the lowest score.
Ben Hogan—on being as.
some tips on winning

Golf is 20 percent talent and 80 percent management.

Ben Hogan

Sometimes we get so stuck on fundamentals and technical thoughts that we forget that the golf ball is simply meant to be projected in a certain direction toward a flag stuck in a hole in the ground.

Peter Jacobsen

Wind, hole design, and a hundred other factors in golf mean that you never hit the same shot two times in a row.

Phil Mickelson

The game was easy for me as a kid, and I had to play a while to find out how hard it is.

Raymond Floyd

I just played crappy, and he played crappy, and I guess he just outcrapped me.
Wayne Grady—on losing to Greg Norman

My game is so bad I gotta hire three caddies—one to walk the left rough, one for the right rough, and one down the middle. And the one in the middle doesn't have much to do.

Dave Hill

Every round I play, I shorten my life by two years.

Tommy Nakajima

I'm playing like Tarzan and hitting like Jane.

Chi Chi Rodriguez

n usually like a yo-yo out there. I play good and then I play bad and then I play good.

Juli Inkster

I'm the best striker of the ball the world has ever known. That's not me saying it. Ask all the pros who's the best. Not the best player, the best striker of the ball.

Moe Norman

The Tour is not what most people seem to think. It's not all sunshine and pretty girls and cheering crowds. It's life without roots. It's a potentially rewarding life but also a frustrating life. There's no real opponent except your own stupid mental and physical mistakes.

Frank Beard

I'm just myself and I hope that's good enough. I've given up trying to be somebody else. I've found out what works for me. And what works for me is just being Payne Stewart.

Payne Stewart

I think that, in golf, your physical and mental capabilities aren't really compatible until you're 35 to 45 ... When you're young, you're blessed with strength and raw ability, but unfortunately, you don't have brain one to go with it. I can't hit it 300 yards in the air anymore, but I've learned a lot of the little things. In the last few years, everything in my game has started complementing everything else.

Raymond Floyd—at age 46

When they start hitting back at you, it's time to quit.
Henry Ransom—after a ball ricocheted off a cliff and hit him

Retire to what? I'm a golfer and a fisherman. I've got no place to retire to.
Julius Boros

Senior Class

Why should I play against those flat bellies when I can play against these round bellies?

Lee Trevino—on why he joined the Senior Tour

Reporters used to ask me questions about the condition of my game. Now all they want to know is about the condition of my health.

Jack Nicklaus

As I've gotten older, I've realized the importance of hanging on to the strength that I've developed.

Gary Player

The young player has strength and energy but envies the experiences of the older player.

Gary Player

The talent was a hell of a lot better than I thought ... I spent a lot of my time preparing for the Seniors out of fear—fear of failure.

Arnold Palmer

When I'm coming down the last nine holes in contention in a Senior event, I feel just as wrapped up in it as I ever did in any tournament.

Arnold Palmer

His nerve, his memory, and I can't remember the third thing.

Lee Trevino—on being asked what three things an aging golfer loses

I tell you, this Senior Tour is a bloody joy.

Gary Player

I never thought I'd wish for my fiftieth birthday to come, but I was counting the days, champing at the bit. I feel like I've been reborn. I'm having a ball.

Bruce Crampton

It reminds you that this really is the Senior Tour.
> *Billy Casper—after Don January collapsed with the flu (he was okay)*

You're never too old to play golf. If you can walk, you can play.
> *Louise Suggs*

Golf is the only game I know of where, as you get to Senior status, you can make adjustments that enable you to keep up with the youngsters.
> *Gary Player*

You know this is the Senior Tour when your back goes out more than you do.
> *Bob Bruce*

They keep talking about the Big Four—Palmer, Nicklaus, Player, and Trevino. I just want to be the fifth wheel in case somebody gets a flat.
> *Chi Chi Rodriguez—on the Senior Tour*

When you get up there in years, the fairways get longer and the holes get smaller.
> *Bobby Locke*

That's the easiest 69 I ever made.
> *Walter Hagen—on turning age 69*

Keep playing.
> *Sam Snead—his advice in a nutshell to seniors*

Tips

Forget your opponents; always play against par.

Sam Snead

Through years of experience I have found that air offers less resistance than dirt.

Jack Nicklaus

Every good player steps up to a shot knowing exactly how he's going to hit the ball.

Tommy Armour

If you can afford only one lesson, tell the pro you want it on the fundamentals: the grip, the stance, and the alignment.

Nancy Lopez

A man who can putt is a match for anyone.

Willie Park

The best single piece of advice I could give any man starting out for a round of golf would be "Take your time," not in studying the ground and lining up the shot, but in swinging the club.

Bobby Jones

I don't really believe there is an orthodox golf swing.

Gary Player

Every golfer scores better when he learns his capabilities.

Tommy Armour

The first thing I learned was to swing hard, and never mind where it went.

Jack Nicklaus

Whenever I mis-hit a shot or notice a swing problem, I return to the basics of swing, stance, grip, and alignment.

Kathy Whitworth

Is there such a thing as a technically perfect swing? If there is, I have yet to see it.

David Leadbetter

You've got to learn to have a relationship with the club head, to know where it's going and what it's doing, and how it's positioned throughout the swing. But most of all, most of all, you've got to feel the club.

Jim Flick, golf coach

Action before thought is the ruination of most of your shots.

Tommy Armour

I want to make this game easy. That one idea—improving my swing—is a simplifying principle. It eliminates a lot of clutter, a lot of false issues.

Tom Watson

Staying in the present is the key to any golfer's game: once you start thinking about a shot you just messed up or what you have to do on the next nine to catch somebody, you're lost.

Paul Azinger

Hit against a firm left side, but hit with the right side.

Calvin Peete

You have to get yourself together, plan your shot, and trust your swing.

Ken Venturi

Addressing the ball in the proper position is the most important fundamental because it determines the kind of swing you will make.

Peter Thomson

Technique is not important to me. I need the same feel and the same swing. That is an advantage, because when you start analyzing, it is confusing.

Nancy Lopez

When you talk turkey with a businessman, you must look squarely at him during the entire conversation. It's the same in putting.

Gene Sarazen

I have proved to myself what I have always said—that a good golfer doesn't have to be born that way. He can be made. I was, and practice is what made me—practice and tough, unrelenting labor.

Ben Hogan

Being left-handed is a big advantage. No one knows enough about your swing to mess you up with advice.

Bob Charles

Lack of versatility in the ways you can work the ball is a killer.

Corey Pavin

As you read greens, remember: First sight is best sight.

Charlie Epps, golf coach

It is utterly impossible for any golfer to play good golf without a swing that will repeat.

Ben Hogan

If you don't set up correctly, it is impossible to improve. Impossible.

Deane Beman

Think about one hip and they both will turn correctly.

Jack Nicklaus

A tremendous amount of power can be derived from a correct use of the hips, legs, and muscles of the back.

Bobby Jones

In terms of its influence on the golf swing, the pre-shot routine is underestimated—hugely so, in my opinion.

Ernie Els

Develop a consistent pre-shot routine.

Tom Watson

The most important thing in golf is to have the same swing every time.

Gary Player

Most golfers spend their whole lives trying to develop a repeating swing, as if mechanics alone will make them good players. I learned early on there is more to golf than that.

Phil Mickelson

Try to think of your golf swing as an efficient machine.

Julius Boros

The distance your ball travels is governed solely by the amount of power you unleash at impact.

Julius Boros

Foot action is one of the main differences between a good golfer and a duffer.

Sam Snead

Long irons take longer to happen, so ease off and allow the swing to happen.

Corey Pavin

The basic factor in all good golf is the grip. Get it right, and all other progress follows.

Tommy Armour

Gripping your club properly is vitally important.

Julius Boros

If you could have a golfer start his swing without a ball there, then suddenly inject the ball in front of the club in the middle of his downswing, he would probably hit the best shot of his life.

Ken Venturi

I regard keeping the head very steady, if not absolutely stock still, throughout the swing as the bedrock fundamental of golf.

Jack Nicklaus

You cannot correct a fault with a fault. That is why I do not talk about theories, but about fundamentals, and why I always go back to fundamentals.

Ken Venturi

The easiest way to learn to play is through imitation.

Beth Daniel

Never imitate.

Bobby Jones

Correct clubface aim is vital to accurate golf shots ... Another crucial element of a good set-up is your posture.

Ernie Els

To me the legs and body are the engine of the golf swing; they fuel and drive it. The arms are simply connecting rods to the club. I regard the hands as linkage hinges through which power, first as leverage and then as centrifugal force, is transmitted to the club head.

Jack Nicklaus

A good player corrects his game by being conscious of his swing. A poor player remains a poor player because he is conscious only of the ball.

Ken Venturi

Two things sadly neglected by the average golfer are footwork and body movement.

Bobby Jones

Strategizing in golf is about seizing every advantage within the rules and etiquette of the game.

Jack Nicklaus

Trust your muscles and hit the ball to the hole. Keep it simple.

Harvey Penick

Long ago I learned that no putt is short enough to take for granted.

Bobby Jones

Treat each putt as a separate little task without worrying about what has gone before or what will come after.

Bernhard Langer

The art of appraising slope and speed—that is, of reading a green—can be derived only from experience.

Bobby Jones

Study the green as you approach it.

Tom Watson

If your fundamentals are solid and you know it, your tempo will be good and stay good, no matter how much pressure is put on it.

Al Geiberger

Golf is a game to be played with two hands. Your left guides the club and keeps the face in the desired position for the hit, and the power pours through the coupling of the right hand and the club.

Tommy Armour

The worst mistake possible in gripping the club is to separate the actions of the two hands.

Bobby Jones

The cardinal principle of all golf shot-making is that if you move your head, you ruin body action.

Tommy Armour

As my hands reach the hitting zone I can increase their speed to anything I choose within my capabilities. So here you have the secret. Turn with your shoulders, hit with your hands.

Julius Boros

The most effective golf is played with a dominant left side.

Carl Lohren

You can tell a good putt by the noise it makes.

Bobby Locke

Develop feel by putting uphill, then downhill.

Tom Watson

When it comes to fundamentals, consistency is paramount.

Greg Norman

You play your best golf by just reacting to the target. If you are focused on the target, you aren't thinking about anything bad happening.

Davis Love III

The positioning of the ball and my alignment are the two areas that my whole swing revolves around.

Ernie Els

The width of the stance is really the foundation of a good swing.

Greg Norman

To swing with power, you've got to think power.

Greg Norman

Every golfer in the world ... can get nothing but good from checking their grip and fundamentals on a regular basis.

Ernie Els

Cultivate a smooth waggle for, as the old Scottish saying goes, "As ye waggle, so shall ye swing."

Tommy Armour

Probably the most important and useful conception for the golfer is that of swinging, ever swinging, as opposed to the idea of forceful hitting.

Bobby Jones

Strive for smoothness, strive for rhythm ...

Bobby Jones

Keep it smooth and slow. Think smoo-oo-ooth.

Larry Nelson

I'm a great believer in the benefits of a balanced, poised finish.

Ernie Els

An angry golfer is a loser. If he can't control himself, he can't control his shots.

Sam Snead

Play with a controlled mad.

Sam Snead

Your mind works best when you're the happiest.

Peter Thomson

Enjoy the game. Happy golf is good golf.

Gary Player

Just relax.

Ernie Els

The Women's Tour

I think I can say with safety that women's championship golf has not only come to stay but that it's sure to keep growing all the way from here on in.

Nancy Lopez

I think it's both thrilling and wonderful to be female, both in being a woman and in being a woman golfer.

Nancy Lopez

When we complain about conditions, we're just bitches. But when the men complain, people think, "Well, it really must be hard."

Betsy King

I love it here in the United States. In Japan, I have no privacy. In the States, I can have a hole in my jeans and nobody will notice.

Ayako Okamoto

Because women are not as strong as men, it's even more important for them to be fundamentally correct in form than it is for men.

Kathy Whitworth

Maybe we need to take a more realistic look at yardages and par for women.

Judy Rankin

What I admire about women amateur golfers is their great ability to switch gears. They have so many things going, so many distractions, and yet most manage to play quite well.

Kathy Whitworth

I'll take a two-shot penalty, but I'll be damned if I'm going to play the ball where it lies.

Elaine Johnson—after her ball bounced off a tree into her bra

I just hitch up my girdle and let 'er fly.

Babe Didrikson Zaharias—on the secret of her driving distance

If I didn't have to worry about these things, I could really hit it a mile.

Babe Didrikson Zaharias—after adjusting her bra

Caddies

Nobody but you and your caddie care what you do out there, and if your caddie is betting against you, he doesn't care either.

Lee Trevino

I've always had confidence, but Roscoe kind of gave me double confidence. Chemistry.

Nancy Lopez—in reference to her caddie, Roscoe Jones

I've been extremely fortunate ... I've had the same great wife since 1976 and the same great caddie since 1978. My caddie, Mike Cowan, certainly knows that my wife is vastly more important to me than he is, and a whole lot better-looking. That said, however, I also feel I've got the best caddie in the business.

Peter Jacobsen—before Cowan went to work for Tiger Woods in 1996

Every golfer has his own quirks, and it's the caddie's job to adapt to them.

Peter Jacobsen

Caddies are a breed of their own. If you shoot a 66, they say, "Man, we shot 66!" But go out and shoot 77, and they say, "Hell, he shot 77!"

Lee Trevino

When I ask you what club to hit, look the other way and don't you dare say a word.

Sam Snead—to his caddie after deciding he'd been relying too much on caddies' bad advice

If each time a player and a caddie split up was actually a divorce, most tour players would have been "married" more times than Zsa Zsa and Liz combined.

Peter Jacobsen

I know you can get fined for throwing a club. What I want to know is if you can get fined for throwing a caddie.

Tommy Bolt

Equipment

Properly fitted clubs are the only part of improved golf that anyone can buy.

Tommy Armour

Perhaps the most important thing I can tell you about equipment is to experiment and keep an open mind.

Gary Player

It may be impractical for women to have golf courses designed for them, but they definitely need—and finally are getting—golf clubs designed for them.

Nancy Lopez

To be a true artist on the greens, you should be as selective in choosing a putter as, say, a master violinist would be in choosing his or her instrument.

Paul Runyan

No game is as exacting as golf in that so many specifications must be met to make a precision fit of implement and player.

Tommy Armour

Don't feel you have to wear a glove for every shot you hit, certainly not just because everyone else at your club probably does.

Ernie Els

Longer clubs won't help a tall golfer.

Jack Nicklaus

In choosing a set of wedges that is right for your game, don't underestimate the value of visual preference. It's a lot easier to have confidence in clubs you like to look at.

Paul Azinger

It's so important to have a putter you feel confident you can hole putts with. It takes pressure off your whole game, and you can just relax and play your best.

Greg Kraft

Those are the times when you look down and stare at your club—as if, for some reason, it was your club's fault instead of your own pathetic swing.

Mark O'Meara—on driving the ball into the water at the U.S. Open

It's a marriage. If I had to choose between my wife and my putter, I'd miss her.

Gary Player

You can't let a putter think it's indispensable. I keep another one—named Number 2—in the car trunk. I switch at least once a year, just to prove to Betsy she can be switched.

Fuzzy Zoeller

Golf is a game that creates emotions that sometimes cannot be sustained with a club in the hand.

Bobby Jones

I broke my toe once by taking an enormous kick at my bag. It was very satisfying—until the point of contact.

David Feherty

The old one didn't float too well.

Craig Stadler—on being asked why he was using a new putter at the 1992 U.S. Open

Fans

I like to sign autographs. I guess I just plain like people.

Arnold Palmer

Part of my philosophy is that a gallery, far from upsetting me, psyches me up.

Nancy Lopez

When you're successful, everybody wants a piece of you.

Lee Trevino

People think I talk in my sleep. I get 'em to think that. I like to give people what they want.

Lee Trevino

I try to be friendly; I give a thousand percent to the public when I'm on the golf course. But when I'm off the course, I like my privacy, and I like it more than most people.

Lee Trevino

To me, the gallery becomes nothing but a wall. I don't even see faces.

Lanny Wadkins

I enjoy the oohs and aahs from the gallery when I hit my drives, but I'm pretty tired of the awws and uhhs when I miss the putts.

John Daly

Without the people, I'd be playing in front of trees for a couple hundred dollars.

Fuzzy Zoeller

It's lonely for most of us out here, even when we're on the course. Nobody cares what you're doing. You can be very successful and nobody knows you. People pay to see Nicklaus. Even if you're in his group and have a huge gallery, hundreds of people are scrambling to the next tee after he putts out—even if you have a three-footer. Face it, you can feel very alone in the middle of a whole lot of people.

Roger Maltbie

Golf has always had the most courteous crowds of any sport, but that's changing. People are realizing they can be heard on television if they're the first ones that yell after a guy hits a shot. We're going to have to get used to it ...

Davis Love III

Putdowns

He is an old man in golf at age 24, has reached his peak and can't get any better. It's a question of how long this boy can hold what he has.

Sam Snead—on Jack Nicklaus, 1965

He was so ugly as a kid, his parents tied pork chops around his neck so that his dog would play with him.

Lee Trevino—on golfer J.C. Snead

There is nothing worse than to find your ball in a hole in the trap, just because some jerk did not take the time to smooth out his footprints or repair his damage.

Gary Player

You've just one problem. You stand too close to the ball—after you hit it.

Sam Snead—giving advice to a student of the game

Ben Crenshaw hits in the woods so often he should get an orange hunting jacket.

Tom Weiskopf

Not bad, but I still prefer golf.

Arnold Palmer—when asked by Frank Sinatra what he thought of Sinatra's game

Miscellaneous Matters

Clothing

In addition to having proper clubs and balls, I feel that to play his best golf a golfer must feel well-dressed.

Gary Player

I even enjoy the mingled pleasure and discomfort of breaking in a new pair of golf shoes.

Arnold Palmer

I remember what interested and impressed me most when I started following Dad and Mom. It was the sound of their golf shoes when they walked on a hard surface like cement. I loved the sound the cleats made, and at the beginning I wanted golf shoes for myself just to walk around in much more than I wanted golf clubs to play with.

Nancy Lopez

Knickers are good for my golf game. They're cooler in hot weather because the air circulates in them, and they're warmer in cold weather because they trap the body heat.

Payne Stewart

Fitness

I really enjoy exercise. Sometimes after a bad day on the course I come home tired and discouraged. But if I exercise before going to bed, I feel clean and strong again. This does wonders for me mentally as well as physically.

Gary Player

Golf is a great game to play when you're pregnant. It's a gentle form of exercise, and if you play regularly it can help you avoid gaining too much weight.

Nancy Lopez

Friendship

Golfers are automatically friends. I can feel comfortable and take intense pleasure playing golf with a president—or a young fellow who supports himself as a busboy.

Arnold Palmer

You find out who your friends are. Some people didn't have much to do with me when I was down. I've got a long memory.

Lanny Wadkins

I play with friends sometimes, but there are never friendly games.

Ben Hogan

Physical Attributes

We always evaluate a player by what the Lord gave him.

Lee Trevino

I have stubby hands with short fingers ... Actually, my wife, Barbara, has stronger hands than mine from doing dishes ... Knowing that, you won't be surprised to learn that I regard as bunk that hoary old maxim about big, strong hands being essential for good golf.

Jack Nicklaus

Greatest pair of hands in golf. The action he gets on his chip shots is almost freakish.

Greg Norman—on Seve Ballesteros

The ideal build for a golfer would be strong hands, big forearms, thin neck, big thighs, and a flat chest. He'd look like Popeye.

Gary Player

Race

Ted Rhodes was the best golfer I ever saw, and that includes Arnold Palmer and Jack Nicklaus. If they ever let him play on the PGA Tour, he would have won everything.

Charlie Sifford—on discrimination during Rhodes's career

I know that in golf I'm a black face walking through a white man's world. It can make you jittery. But I've reached the point I don't feel like an outsider. I know half the people I meet.

Jim Thorpe

It's really nice seeing more minorities in the gallery. I think that's where the game should go and will go.

Tiger Woods

Superstitions

I'm very superstitious. I think everyone is a little bit, but they don't want to admit it.

Chi Chi Rodriguez

If a golfer gets superstitious, he'll only go one way—down. Some players may wear the same shirt for four straight days. No wonder they don't attract much of a gallery.

Gary Player

Star Power

That's life. The older you get, the tougher it is to score.

Bob Hope

Jack Lemmon's been in more bunkers than Eva Braun.

Phil Harris

I've seen better swings on a condemned playgound.

Peter Jacobsen—on Jack Lemmon's swing

My God, he looks like he's beating a chicken.

Byron Nelson—on Jack Lemmon's swing

He hits the ball 130 yards and his jewelry goes 150.

Bob Hope—on Sammy Davis Jr.

He has won almost as much money playing golf as I've spent on lessons.

Bob Hope—on Arnold Palmer

Bob has a beautiful short game. Unfortunately, it's off the tee.

Jimmy Demaret—on Bob Hope

I'll shoot my age if I have to live to be 105.

Bob Hope

Give me good clubs, fresh air and a beautiful partner, and you can keep the clubs and fresh air.

Jack Benny

It took me seventeen years to get 3,000 hits in baseball. I did it in one afternoon on the golf course.

Henry Aaron

Golf is the only sport where the ball doesn't move until you hit it.

Ted Williams

Baseball reveals character; golf exposes it.

Ernie Banks

Ninety percent of putts that are short don't go in.

Yogi Berra

I was three over: one over a house; one over a patio, and one over a swimming pool.

George Brett

If you drink, don't drive. Don't even putt.

Dean Martin

You've heard of Arnie's Army. Well, those are Dean's Drunks.
Dean Martin—on his fans in the gallery

The safest place would be the fairway.
Joe Garagiola—on where the gallery should stand during a celebrity tournament

Prayer never seems to work for me on the golf course. I think this has something to do with my being a terrible putter.

Rev. Billy Graham

A lot more people beat me now.
Dwight Eisenhower—on the changes in his golf game after leaving the White House

Golf is a game whose aim is to hit a very small ball into a very small hole, with weapons singularly ill-designed for that purpose.

Winston Churchill

Some of us worship in churches, some in synagogues, some on golf courses.
Adlai Stevenson

[Richard] Nixon could relate to the ordinary guy who plays. Hell, I even once caught him cheating a little bit—moving the ball when he didn't think nobody could see him. All hackers do that.

Sam Snead

We have fifty-one golf courses in Palm Springs. He never decides which course he will play until after his first tee shot.

Bob Hope—on Gerald Ford

It's not hard to find Gerald Ford on a golf course. Just follow the wounded.

Bob Hope

I'll know I'm getting better at golf because I'm hitting fewer spectators.

Gerald Ford

He told me he caddied in the same group with me in the Hot Springs Open. That's why I voted for him, because he was my caddie.

Tommy Bolt—on Bill Clinton

Golf has made more liars out of people than the income tax.

Will Rogers

Your clubs.

Jackie Gleason—to Toots Shor, on being asked what to give the caddie after Shor shot 211

The reason the pro tells you to keep your head down is so you can't see him laughing.

Phyllis Diller

Golf has taught me there is a connection between pain and pleasure. "Golf" spelled backwards is "flog."

Phyllis Diller

I'll be playing center for the Chicago Bulls before Michael Jordan plays on the Tour.

Peter Jacobsen

Man, the worst thing about this is I won't be able to play golf.
Charles Barkley—on a shoulder injury

The course is the most wonderful combination of beauty and beast.
Jack Lemmon—on Cypress Point

I couldn't tell you exactly what I like about golf. Just when you think you've got it mastered, it lets you know you haven't. I'm just crazy enough to do it.
Clint Eastwood

Par is whatever I say it is. I've got one hole that's a par 23, and yesterday I damn-near birdied the sucker.
Willie Nelson

To really lose weight playing golf, the best place to play is Mexico. Go to any Mexican golf course, stop at every hole, and drink water. Within a week you'll be down to your desired weight.
Buddy Hackett

One minute it's fear and loathing, but hit a couple of good shots and you're on top of the world. I've gone crazy over this game.
Jack Nicholson

Golf is good for the soul. You get so mad at yourself you forget to hate your enemies.
Will Rogers

When is Tiger coming? When is Tiger coming?
Ken Griffey Jr.—on the prospect of
playing a round of golf with Tiger Woods

Amateur Hour

The sport's [golf's] best medium is not television, radio, or the eye. Even more than baseball, it's the sport of words.

Thomas Boswell—writer

The smaller the ball used in the sport, the better the book.

George Plimpton—writer

Golf is the most jealous of mistresses.

Arnold Haultain—writer

Three things that are as unfathomable as they are fascinating to the masculine mind: metaphysics golf and the feminine heart.

Arnold Haultain

He who would attain self-knowledge should frequent the links.

Arnold Haultain

Golf, in short, is not so much a game as it is a creed and a religion.

Arnold Haultain

Golf is a good walk spoiled.

Mark Twain

Golf is the cruelest of sports. Like life, it's unfair. It's a harlot. A trollop. It leads you on. It never lives up to its promises. It's not a sport, it's bondage. An obsession. A boulevard of broken dreams. It plays with men. And runs off with the butcher.

Jim Murray—writer

The first thing any beginning golfer should learn is the code of etiquette.
Edward F. Chui—chairman of the Physical Education
Department at the University of Hawaii

We are finding that many well-managed golf courses harbor a greater diversity of wildlife than many parks and refuges.

Donald G. Dodson—president of the Audubon Society of New York

Magical. That's what St. Andrews is to all lovers of golf or Scotland or both.

Dick Taylor—former editor-in-chief of Golf World

Bobby Jones and St. Andrews: what each meant to the other is one of the greatest love stories in the annals of golf.

Sidney L. Matthew—lawyer and expert on the life of Bobby Jones

Player, Palmer, and Nicklaus, although unlike in style and method, have one thing in common—an aggressive attacking approach to the game.

Geoffrey Cousins—golf historian

In 1940, before America entered the war, the leading money winner, Ben Hogan, amassed just over 10,000 dollars.

Geoffrey Cousins

The crystallization of the dream of an artist who had been drinking gin and sobering up on absinthe.

O.B. Keeler—biographer of Bobby Jones on Cypress Point

Like pool, golf is primarily a game of position. The professional pool player never takes one shot at a time. He organizes a series of shots in his mind in order to sink all the balls on the table. The key is to get a good "leave" or an ideal position for the next shot.

Robert Trent Jones, Jr.—designer of golf courses

Golf courses provide a great habitat for wildlife, buffer zones to developed areas, storm water control, green space, noise abatement, dust control, cooling—in short, properly managed golf courses are good for the environment.

Dr. Thomas L. Watschke—writer

Hazards are like spices that a designer sprinkles on a course to give it flavor.

Robert Trent Jones, Jr.

Golf is not, on the whole, a game for realists. By its exactitudes of measurement it invites the attention of perfectionists.

Heywood Hale Broun—writer

Every hacker's problem—is not that we are inherently bad golfers; it's that we are inherently bad people, and therefore unable to play good golf. It's an interesting twist on Original Sin ...

Glen Waggoner—writer

I like golf because you can be really terrible at it and still not look much dorkier than anybody else.

Dave Barry—humorist

Eventually all golfers suffer a nervous collapse.

Stephen Baker—writer

The most exquisitely satisfying act in the world of golf is that of throwing a club. The full backswing, the delayed wrist action, the flowing follow-through, followed by that unique whirring sound, reminiscent only of a flock of passing starlings, is without parallel in the sport.

Henry Longhurst—writer

I don't deserve any credit. God had already done 90 percent of the work.

Peter Dye—designer of golf courses, on Kiawah Island

Golf is not a fair game, so why build a course fair?

Peter Dye

To find a man's true character, play golf with him,

P.G. Wodehouse—writer

There are three rules for a caddie to live by: show up, keep up, shut up.

Paul Jungman—caddie

Golf is so popular simply because it is the best game in the world in which to be bad.

A.A. Milne—writer

Many recognize that golf is largely a mental game and that mastery of the mind while golfing will lead to great results.

Leland T. Lewis—writer

The first dedicated woman golfer was credited to be Mary Queen of Scots ... So enthralled was she with the game that in 1567 she was spotted on the links just three days after her husband's murder.

David G. Marrandette—writer

The way Betsy is playing, Rin Tin Tin could carry her clubs and it wouldn't make any difference.

Gary Harrison—Betsy King's caddie on her way to the 1991 LPGA Championship

When you are ahead, don't take it easy, kill them. After the finish, then be a sportsman.

Earl Woods—to his son Tiger Woods

Golf is 20 percent mechanics and technique. The other 80 percent is philosophy, humor, tragedy, romance, melodrama, companionship, camaraderie, cussedness and conversation.

Grantland Rice—writer

Out of the mouths of America's most clean-cut group of athletes, except perhaps bowlers, comes a rich vein of slang that makes the hyped-up wild men of the NFL seem bland.

Thomas Boswell—writer on golfers

On the golf course as nowhere else, the tyranny of causality is suspended, and men are free.

John Updike—writer

The Future

To look out here and see so many kids, I think that's wonderful. They see someone they can relate to, me being so young.

Tiger Woods